EXPLORE
RIVERS AND PONDS!

CARLA MOONEY
Illustrated by Bryan Stone

Nomad Press is committed to preserving ancient forests and natural resources. We elected to print *Explore Rivers and Ponds!* on 30% post consumer recycled paper, processed chlorine free.

As a result, for this printing, we have saved:

- 10 Trees (40' tall and 6-8" diameter)
- 4,526 Gallons of Wastewater
- 4 million BTU's of Total Energy
- 286 Pounds of Solid Waste
- 1,004 Pounds of Greenhouse Gases

Nomad Press made this paper choice because our printer, Thomson-Shore, Inc., is a member of Green Press Initiative, a nonprofit program dedicated to supporting authors, publishers, and suppliers in their efforts to reduce their use of fiber obtained from endangered forests. For more information, **visit www.greenpressinitiative.org.**

Environmental impact estimates were made using the Environmental Defense Paper Calculator. For more information visit: www.papercalculator.org.

Nomad Press
A division of Nomad Communications
10 9 8 7 6 5 4 3 2 1

Manufactured by Thomson-Shore, Dexter, MI (USA)
August 2012, RMA583HS292
ISBN: 978-1-93674-980-5

Illustrations by Bryan Stone
Educational Consultant, Marla Conn

Questions regarding the ordering of this book should be addressed to
Independent Publishers Group
814 N. Franklin St.
Chicago, IL 60610
www.ipgbook.com

Nomad Press
2456 Christian St.
White River Junction, VT 05001
www.nomadpress.net

CONTENTS

Titles in the **Explore Your World!** Series

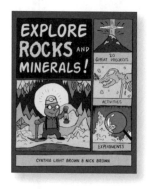

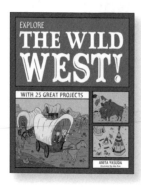

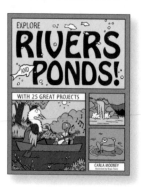

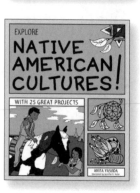

The World of Water

Have you ever looked at a map of the earth, or a **globe**? You've probably noticed that a lot of our planet is covered in water. Most of this is salt water in the oceans. Only about 3 percent of the earth's water is fresh. And of that very small amount, most is solid ice in **glaciers** or hidden deep underground.

Because so much **freshwater** is frozen or hard to reach, it can't be used by humans, animals, or plants. In fact, the freshwater we can use covers only a tiny part of the earth's surface. Think of it this way: if all the water in the world were the size of a globe, the freshwater we can use would be just a tiny drop about the size of a marble.

1

WORDS to KNOW

bog: an area of wet, spongy land that is full of **peat**.

peat: dark brown, partly decayed plant matter found in bogs and swamps.

amphibian: an animal with a backbone that lives on land and in water, such as a frog, toad, or salamander. An amphibian is cold-blooded, so it needs sunlight to keep warm and shade to keep cool.

ecosystem: a community of living and nonliving things and their **environment**. Living things are plants, animals, and insects. Nonliving things are soil, rocks, and water.

environment: a natural area with animals, plants, rocks, soil, and water.

habitat: the natural area where a plant or animal lives.

So what exactly is freshwater? It's water that is not salty. Freshwater is found in many different places that are called bodies of water. Lakes, streams, ponds, brooks, creeks, rivers, **bogs**, marshes, and even a tiny puddle on your driveway are all freshwater.

What's the big deal about freshwater? It is important because wherever you find freshwater, you'll find life! Some of these forms of life are big enough for you to see. Others are so tiny you need a microscope to see them. But they're in there.

A wide variety of animals, birds, **amphibians**, insects, and plants make their homes in or near freshwater **ecosystems**. Every freshwater **habitat** holds a world of wacky, weird, and wonderful life. In fact, freshwater is such a great place to live that more living things make their home in freshwater than anywhere else on Earth.

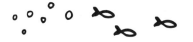

You use freshwater every day. You drink freshwater. You use it to take a bath or shower. If you help your parents to water houseplants or a garden, you are using freshwater to keep the plants alive. You even use freshwater to flush your toilets!

WORDS to KNOW

pollute: to make dirty or contaminate.

groundwater: water that is underground in spaces between rocks.

In this book, you'll explore all types of freshwater bodies and habitats. You'll learn how each is formed. You'll see what types of plants and animals make their homes there. And you'll find out what happens when something **pollutes** or disrupts these freshwater habitats.

Did You Know?

There is more freshwater stored as **groundwater** than the total amount of water found in lakes and rivers.

The Freshwater Biome

WORDS to KNOW

wetland: an area where the land is soaked with water, such as a **swamp**.

swamp: an area of wet, spongy ground that grows woody plants like trees and shrubs.

biome: a large area with a similar climate, and the plants and animals that live there.

Freshwater ecosystems are everywhere you look. These ecosystems include lakes, ponds, rivers, streams, and **wetlands**. In fact, any pool of water that is mostly salt-free can be called a freshwater ecosystem, even one that is only up to your ankles. Freshwater ecosystems can exist in puddles, ditches, and gutters. Together, freshwater ecosystems, large and small, make up Earth's freshwater **biome**. So where does all this freshwater come from? And why isn't it salty?

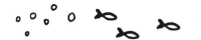 

WORDS to KNOW

water cycle: the natural recycling of water through evaporation, condensation, precipitation, and collection.

evaporation: when a liquid heats up and changes to a gas.

condensation: when a gas cools and changes to a liquid.

precipitation: falling moisture in the form of rain, sleet, snow, and hail.

collection: when water that falls back to Earth is stored on land or in oceans, ponds, rivers, lakes, and streams.

The Water Cycle

Did you know that there is no new supply of freshwater on Earth? It can be hard to believe, but the same freshwater has been used and reused for millions of years. All life on Earth depends on this process, called the **water cycle**.

The water cycle has four major parts, which include **evaporation**, **condensation**, **precipitation**, and **collection**. Water is constantly moving through these four processes. It is always changing form, from liquid to gas, maybe to ice, and back again.

CONDENSATION

PRECIPITATION

EVAPORATION

COLLECTION

EVAPORATION. You may have noticed that puddles on the ground disappear after some time. This happens when the water evaporates into the air. When water changes from its liquid form into a gas called **water vapor**, it has evaporated. Heat from the sun can speed up evaporation, just like a tea kettle on the stove turns heated water into steam. Water will evaporate more quickly in hot areas than in cold areas.

In the water cycle, the sun warms water in oceans and in freshwater bodies such as lakes and rivers. Some of that water evaporates into the air. Water also enters the air from the leaves of trees and plants. This process is called **transpiration**.

water vapor: the gas form of water.

transpiration: when plants give off moisture into the air.

atmosphere: the air surrounding the earth.

WORDS to **KNOW**

CONDENSATION. When water changes into water vapor, it rises into the air. The wind spreads the water vapor throughout the **atmosphere**. As the water vapor rises higher, it cools. When the water vapor cools, it turns back into a liquid. This is condensation, the opposite of evaporation. Think about a cold glass of ice water on a hot day. Tiny beads of water form on the outside of your glass. This happens when water vapor in the air touches the cold glass. The vapor cools and turns into the drops of liquid water on your glass.

PRECIPITATION. Condensing water vapor forms tiny water droplets. These combine with dust particles to form clouds. Some areas have more clouds than others. If you live near a large lake, you will see more clouds than if you live near the desert, because there is more water vapor in the air.

When the tiny water droplets in clouds get too heavy, they fall to the ground as precipitation. Moisture that falls from the sky can fall as rain, snow, sleet, or hail. Most of the time, precipitation falls as raindrops.

COLLECTION. All that precipitation lands and gets collected somewhere on Earth. Most falls back into the oceans. Some **flows** over land and down hills into freshwater rivers, lakes, ponds, and streams as **surface runoff**. The rest soaks into the ground. Water that stays underground is called groundwater. As water soaks through the ground, soil and rocks filter out **impurities** and help clean the water. Groundwater can be stored for long periods.

Eventually, this collected water evaporates and the whole water cycle begins again.

WORDS to KNOW

flow: to move from one place to another.

surface runoff: water that stays on the surface and flows into streams, rivers, lakes, and oceans.

impurity: contamination or **pollution**.

pollution: harmful materials that damage the air, water, and soil. These include chemicals and factory waste.

Life in Freshwater

Wherever you have freshwater, life will come. An incredible variety of animals and plants make their homes in the freshwater biome. That's because this biome provides the **nutrients** to feed all the **organisms** living there.

Many types of fish, birds, insects, amphibians, and **crustaceans** live in freshwater. Plants such as **algae** and grasses like cattails grow in and near ponds and **marshes**. Snapping turtles and mallard ducks swim in ponds. Crayfish, shrimp, and tadpoles live deep in swamps. Catfish, carp, and salmon swim in rivers and streams. Larger animals like beavers and otters make their homes both in the water and on the land around it. Other **mammals** live near the water and use it for drinking.

WORDS to **KNOW**

nutrients: the substances found in food that organisms need to live and grow.

organism: any living thing.

crustacean: a type of animal, such as a crab or lobster, that lives mainly in water. It has several pairs of legs and its body is made up of sections covered in a hard outer shell.

algae: a simple organism found in water that is like a plant but without roots, stems, or leaves.

marsh: an inland area of wet, low land.

mammal: a type of animal, such as a human, dog, or cat. Mammals are born live, feed milk to their young, and usually have hair or fur covering most of their skin.

Did You Know?

Rain isn't salty because when ocean water evaporates the salt stays in the ocean. So the water vapor that continues through the water cycle is not salty. When this freshwater comes back to Earth as precipitation, some ends up rivers, streams, lakes, and ponds. Without any salt, these bodies of water stay fresh.

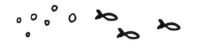

WORDS to KNOW

food chain: a community of plants and animals, where each is eaten by another higher up in the chain.

phytoplankton: tiny free-floating plants and plant-like organisms.

photosynthesis: the process where plants use sunlight and water to make their own food.

primary producer: a plant that creates its own food for energy through photosynthesis.

zooplankton: tiny animals that float freely in salt water and freshwater.

primary consumer: a plant or animal that eats tiny plants and phytoplankton.

Food Chains: Linked Together

Life in a freshwater biome is connected like links on a chain. From the tiniest algae to the largest animal, each link in the **food chain** is important. The first link is the food chain's energy source: the sun. When sunlight hits plants and **phytoplankton**, these organisms create the energy they need to grow and live. This process is called **photosynthesis**. Phytoplankton and plants are **primary producers** that make their own food, instead of eating it like you do.

The next link in the food chain happens when tiny animals called **zooplankton** eat phytoplankton. Most zooplankton, except jellyfish, are so small that you need a microscope to see one. Animals like zooplankton that eat primary producers are called **primary consumers**.

Did You Know?

If all the water vapor in the air fell at once, the earth would be covered with only about 1 inch of water (2½ centimeters).

9

secondary consumer: an animal that eats other animals.

food web: a network of connected food chains.

The freshwater food chain keeps growing. Small fish and insects eat zooplankton. Then larger fish eat the insects and smaller fish. Animals that eat other animals are called **secondary consumers**. Each connection is another link in the food chain. A simple freshwater food chain might connect like this:

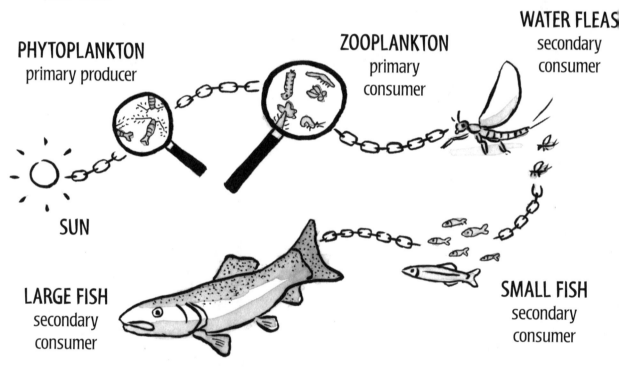

PHYTOPLANKTON
primary producer

ZOOPLANKTON
primary consumer

WATER FLEAS
secondary consumer

SUN

LARGE FISH
secondary consumer

SMALL FISH
secondary consumer

Food chains are not always so simple. Many animals eat more than one type of food. Some animals eat one food when they are young and switch to another food source as adults. When several food chains are connected, they become a **food web**.

The Circle of Life

Eventually, all living things die. When plants and animals die, **scavengers** and **decomposers** break down their bodies. First, scavengers eat pieces of the dead animal or plant. Then, decomposers feed on what's left and pass along the nutrients to the soil. These nutrients get absorbed by plants in the freshwater biome and the food chain starts again!

WORDS to KNOW

scavenger: an animal, like a vulture or hyena, that feeds on dead and rotting organisms.

decomposer: an organism, like a worm or ant, that breaks down dead and rotting organisms.

waterfowl: a bird that lives on freshwater lakes and streams.

Animals in Ponds & Rivers: Birds

Ponds and rivers attract birds. You can often see **waterfowl** like swans, geese, and ducks swimming in these bodies of water. Their heavy bodies and webbed feet help them swim, and they use their long, flexible necks to dunk their heads underwater to find plants and animals to eat. During the spring, the plants around the pond and river's edge are a good place for waterfowl to build a safe nest. In the winter, when the ponds and rivers freeze, many fly south to warmer places.

Many other birds gather near ponds and rivers to drink and to eat plants, waterweeds, fish, frogs, and insects. Birds such as the brightly colored kingfisher dive for fish. Others, like the heron, live in ponds, marshes, and rivers and hunt fish and frogs with their spear-like bills. Some birds, like the warblers, build their nests and raise their young in the grasses and mosses found near ponds and rivers.

11

From the tiniest phytoplankton to the largest mammal, plants and animals in the freshwater biome are connected. Yet not all freshwater habitats are the same. They vary in temperature and conditions. Some, such as lakes and ponds, have calm, still waters. Others, such as rivers and streams, have constantly flowing **currents**.

Plants and animals have **adapted** over time to live in the different freshwater habitats. Plants that live in rivers need strong roots to survive the flowing water. Certain fish, such as carp, prefer to feed from the bottom of a still pond instead of a moving stream. Despite their differences, each freshwater habitat is an amazing, connected web of life.

WORDS to KNOW

current: the steady movement of water in one direction.

adapt: changes a plant or animal makes to live in new or different conditions.

Did You Know?

An ecologist is a scientist who studies how organisms interact with the other plants and animals in their habitats.

12

Play the
Food Chain Game

A food chain is a community of plants and animals, where each is eaten by another higher up in the chain. Play this game to make your own freshwater food chain.

1 Write each of the following on a separate index card: Plants, Grasshopper, Owl, Snake, Sun, Frog. Draw pictures of the plants and animals on each card.

2 What eats what? See if you can put the food chain in order.

3 Try the game again, this time using your own animals and plants from a freshwater biome.

CLASSROOM CONNECTION: Talk with your class about what would happen to the plants and animals in the food chain if you took one card away. What if you took two away?

Make Your Own
Freshwater

The water cycle takes salt water from the ocean and turns it into freshwater. When the salt water evaporates, it leaves the salt in the ocean. When the water vapor cools and turns into rain, it falls as freshwater! This is how rain fills lakes and rivers with freshwater. In this activity, you can explore how the water cycle turns salt water into fresh!

SUPPLIES

- 2 cups water (470 milliliters)
- large glass bowl
- 3 teaspoons salt (15 milliliters)
- spoon
- ceramic mug or cup
- plastic wrap
- large rubber band
- sunlight
- small rock

1 Pour the water into a large bowl and add the salt. Stir with the spoon.

2 Place the ceramic cup in the middle of the bowl of water. Make sure the water in the bowl is below the top of the cup.

Did You Know?

When water from lakes, rivers, and ponds evaporates into the air, it leaves behind any impurities. This makes the water vapor cleaner than it was on Earth!

3 Cover the bowl with plastic wrap and seal it tightly with a rubber band.

4 Put your bowl in a safe place that gets lots of sunshine, such as a window sill. Place a small rock on top of the plastic, directly over the cup.

5 After several hours, condensation should form on the underside of the plastic wrap. Drops of water should flow slowly downward into your cup. Check your cup. If it has water in it, you can drink it. It is now salt-free!

HOW IT WORKS: The sun's heat causes the water to evaporate into a gas. The salt stays in the glass bowl. When the evaporated water cools, it turns back into liquid. It becomes condensation on the plastic. The freshwater then runs down the plastic, into the cup!

Try a
Water Cycle Experiment

You can watch the water cycle in action in a terrarium. This is a miniature garden in a jar. Plants give off water vapor into the air. The jar traps the water vapor. The vapor condenses and runs down the sides of the jar. It returns as water droplets to the soil. The plants use the water in the soil.

SUPPLIES

- ⊙ glass jar
- ⊙ small rocks
- ⊙ sand
- ⊙ soil
- ⊙ small green plants
- ⊙ bottle cap
- ⊙ water
- ⊙ plastic wrap

1 Line the bottom of your jar with small rocks. Then put about an inch or two of sand on top of the rocks (2½ to 5 centimeters).

2 Add a couple inches of soil on top of the sand (about 5 centimeters).

3 Put the green plants in the soil on one side of the jar. Fill the bottle cap with water and place it on the other side of the jar.

4 Cover the jar opening with plastic wrap and put it in a sunny spot.

5 Watch as the water cycle works before your eyes, making your plants grow!

Make Your Own
Dipping Net

When you go on a field trip to a pond, stream, or wetland, you can use a dipping net to see what creatures you find living there. **Have an adult help you with this project.**

SUPPLIES

- ⊙ wire coat hanger
- ⊙ scissors
- ⊙ sheer nylons or tights
- ⊙ needle and thread
- ⊙ stick or rod
- ⊙ string or duct tape

1 Bend the coat hanger into a square shape.

2 Cut the tights about halfway down the two legs. Using the piece with the waistband attached, tie the legs together. This will form a basket for the net.

3 Put the tights inside the coat hanger square. Fold the waistband over the coat hanger so that the hem is on the outside of the net.

4 Use a needle and thread to sew the waistband over the coat hanger. This will hold the tights to the coat hanger.

5 Tie or tape the coat hanger's hook end to the stick or rod with string or duct tape.

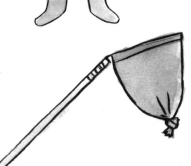

Assemble an Ecologist's Field Kit

Ecologists teach others about the natural world we live in. Many ecologists study freshwater ponds, lakes, rivers, streams, and wetlands. They visit ponds and rivers to observe the animals and plants living there. They conduct experiments to learn more about the habitat. When visiting a lake or river, ecologists usually bring tools and supplies to help them in their research.

SUPPLIES

- several glass or plastic jars with lids
- dipping net
- magnifying glass
- bug card (from activity on page 37)
- spiral notebook
- markers
- stickers
- pencil
- rubber boots
- backpack or sturdy bag

You can assemble your own ecologist's field kit to take on your next field trip to a pond or stream.

1 Gather your supplies.

- **Jars** to hold samples of soil, water, plants, or animal life.

- **Dipping net** to scoop samples of water from ponds, rivers, and wetlands.

- **Magnifying glass** to see small insects, creatures, and plants.

- **Bug card** to identify insects that you find near a freshwater body. You will make this in the next chapter.

- **Spiral notebook** to write down what you see, hear, and smell. Decorate the cover with markers and stickers and label it your "Freshwater Journal."

- **Pencil**

- **Rubber boots** to keep your feet dry.

2 Place the items carefully in your backpack or sturdy bag.

3 Now you're ready for a freshwater field trip. Dig in and get messy!

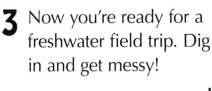

Examine Life in a
Puddle

Even a small puddle is part of the freshwater biome. In a puddle, you may find tiny water fleas, small amphibians like toads, mosquito **larvae**, or insects like the water boatman. Try making your own puddle and seeing what life comes to live in it. **Have an adult supervise your Internet research.**

SUPPLIES

- ⊙ large bucket or plastic tub
- ⊙ water
- ⊙ magnifying glass
- ⊙ Freshwater Journal
- ⊙ pencil
- ⊙ Internet access or nature field guide

1 Fill your bucket or tub with water and place it outside in a safe place where it will not be disturbed.

2 Leave your bucket outside for several weeks. Check it each week. What do you see in the water? You may need to use a magnifying glass to see the tiniest creatures.

WORDS to KNOW

larva: the wormlike stage of an insect's life. The plural is larvae.

3 Record what you see in your Freshwater Journal. Draw pictures of anything that you find.

4 Have an adult help you research what you've found on the Internet or in a nature field guide. What is it?

Ponds and Lakes

A body of freshwater surrounded by land is a pond or lake. Ponds and lakes come in many sizes. A tiny pond can be as small as a few square yards (a few square meters). A great lake can stretch as far as you can see and beyond. While water in a river or stream is always moving from one place to another, the water in ponds and lakes can be still.

Ponds

You can find ponds all around you. They are in parks and neighborhoods. You might even have a pond in your own backyard. Whenever something makes a shallow hole in the ground and water pools up in it, a pond is born!

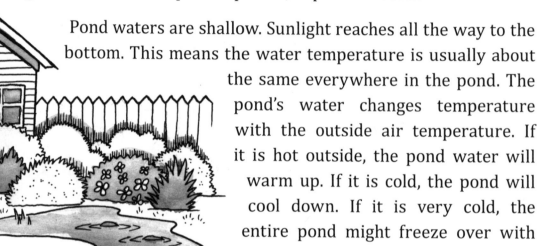

Pond waters are shallow. Sunlight reaches all the way to the bottom. This means the water temperature is usually about the same everywhere in the pond. The pond's water changes temperature with the outside air temperature. If it is hot outside, the pond water will warm up. If it is cold, the pond will cool down. If it is very cold, the entire pond might freeze over with ice and you can skate on it.

Lake or Pond?

How do you tell the difference between a lake and a pond? If you are looking at an enormous lake or a tiny pond, the answer is easy. But what if you are looking at something in the middle? Most people use depth and size to decide if a body of water is a lake or pond. When the water is shallow and the sunlight reaches the bottom of all areas in the water, it's a pond. If there are areas that are too deep for sunlight to reach the bottom, it's a lake. You can also look at how large the surface of the water is. Ponds usually have small surface areas. Lakes have large surface areas. So you decide. Is it a lake or pond?

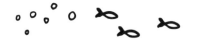 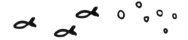

WORDS to KNOW

decompose: to rot or decay.

debris: the scattered pieces of something that has been broken or destroyed.

Sometimes ponds dry up and disappear. How does this happen?

Many different plants grow in and around ponds. When plants die, new plants take their place. As the dead plants **decompose**, they leave a layer of dirt and **debris** on the bottom of the pond. This layer keeps building up.

Eventually, the pond's bottom is close enough to the surface that the plants spread across the top of the water. When this happens, the pond's shallow, muddy waters become a marsh. As the marsh fills with more dirt and debris, trees may grow. It becomes a swamp. Over more years, the shallow swamp may dry out until the pond finally disappears.

Ponds are a great place to find animals and plants. Visit a pond and you might see frogs, fish, insects, and turtles. These creatures feed, find shelter, and raise their young by the pond. Some animals also drop seeds around the pond. The seeds grow into the pond's plants. Because a pond's water is still, the plants do not need strong roots to survive.

Reeds, **rushes**, and many other plants grow in the wet soil around ponds. Other plants have adapted to life in the freshwater itself. Waterweeds grow completely under the water. Sometimes, if you dive down, you can see a tiny underwater forest. The weeds provide food and shelter for animals that live in the water.

WORDS to KNOW

rush: a tall plant with a hollow stem that grows in wet places like ponds and marshes.

emergent: a plant that is rooted in soil but has plant parts that reach above the surface of the water.

Other plants called **emergents** have roots in the watery mud, but their flowers and leaves float on the surface. Water lilies with their beautiful flowers and round leaves are a common emergent in ponds and lakes. And animals and insects need them. Snails lay their eggs on the undersides of the lily pad. Frogs rest on lily pads and wait to snatch a nearby fly for lunch.

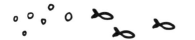

Some freshwater plants like duckweed and water ferns are not rooted in the mud at the bottom of the pond or lake. Instead, they float over the surface of the water. Their roots trail along and absorb **minerals** from the water. Duckweed is one of the simplest floating plants. It grows flowers in shallow water that receives plenty of sunlight. The plant's leaves have air-filled spaces called lacunae that make the plant light enough to float on the water's surface.

WORDS to KNOW

mineral: something found in nature that is not an animal or plant, like gold, salt, or copper.

watershed: the land area that drains into a river or a lake.

Lakes

Like a pond, a lake is a body of freshwater that is not flowing. Lakes are bigger and deeper than ponds. Some lakes are big enough to have waves and can look like the ocean. A lake forms where surface water gathers in a large, low area in the ground. Lakes collect water that falls in the area and travels down through the **watershed**.

WORDS to KNOW

landslide: when rocks and soil slide down a mountain.

meteorite: a piece of rock from outer space that falls to Earth.

crater: a large hole in the ground caused by something like a meteorite or a bomb.

erosion: the gradual wearing away of soil by water or wind.

oxbow lake: a horseshoe-shaped lake that starts out as a curve in a river. It becomes a lake next to the river when the river changes its **course**.

course: the path of a river or stream.

Some lakes form naturally. Picture a glacier moving down the side of a mountain. As it moves, it builds up large piles of rock and soil. Lakes form behind these piles. Sometimes pieces of ice fall off the main glacier. When the ice melts, a lake forms. Glaciers have formed some of the world's largest lakes, including the Great Lakes in the United States.

Other times, changes in the earth's surface cause areas to fill with water. A **landslide** can leave rocks and soil that cut off part of a river and create a large lake. Some lakes form quickly when a **meteorite** hits the earth. The impact leaves a **crater** that fills with water. Other lakes form gradually, when **erosion** slowly creates a sunken place in the ground. U-shaped **oxbow lakes** form when a curve of a river is cut off from the main channel.

Did You Know?

Lake Baikal in Russia is the largest freshwater lake in the world. It contains 20 percent of the world's fresh surface water.

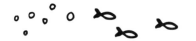

WORDS to KNOW

dam: a strong barrier built across a stream or river to hold back water.

Other lakes are manmade. Sometimes, people build **dams** across a river to control the water flow. The water trapped behind the dam forms a lake.

Lakes and rivers often work together. Some lakes are the source of water for rivers. The mighty Mississippi River begins at Lake Itasca in Minnesota. Many important rivers start in a lake. Other rivers empty into a lake. The Niagara River, which flows along the border of Canada and New York, empties into Lake Ontario. Because lakes and rivers often share waters, many of the same animals and plants live in both places.

The Great Lakes

On the border of Canada and the United States, the Great Lakes are the largest group of freshwater lakes in the world. There are five Great Lakes: Lake Superior, Lake Michigan, Lake Huron, Lake Erie, and Lake Ontario. These five lakes hold 90 percent (almost all!) of the freshwater in the United States. They hold 21 percent of the supply of fresh surface water in the entire world, and half of that is stored in Lake Superior. Lake Superior holds enough water to fill all the other Great Lakes three times over!

27

Lakes are an important part of our world. They provide a place for fish, animals, and tiny water creatures to live. They are a place for dirt and **sediments** to settle and spread out. By providing a place for water to gather, lakes help control floods. People also use lakes for recreation and relaxation.

Stratification—A Lake's Layers

Because lakes can be deep, the water temperature is not the same all the way to the bottom. This is part of what makes a lake different from a pond. Lakes have different layers of water that are different temperatures. This temperature difference is called **stratification**. The temperatures of the layers change with the seasons. Sometimes the warmer water is on the surface, and sometimes it is deeper down.

A Place To Live

Ponds and lakes are full of plant and animal life. Plants provide food and shelter for many animals. Crayfish, salamanders, and newts crawl in the shallow water. Ducks and insects live above the water. Other animals, like raccoons, live on the ground near the water. Because ponds and lakes are so crowded, plants and animals compete for space and food.

28

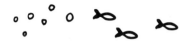 

Have you ever waded into a lake in the summer and noticed that as you went deeper, your feet felt colder near the bottom than your shoulders felt near the top? In summer, the cooler water sinks to the bottom of the lake. Many of the lake's creatures live in the water's upper layer because it is warmer and has more food.

WORDS to KNOW

hibernate: to spend the winter in a deep sleep.

As the air starts to get colder in the fall, the lake's top layer cools. The water becomes almost the same temperature from top to bottom. Then fish and other lake animals swim and live in all of the lake's layers.

But when winter comes, things change. Cold winter winds chill the top layer of water more than the lake's bottom layer. So it is warmer at the bottom. The fish swim far below the surface of the

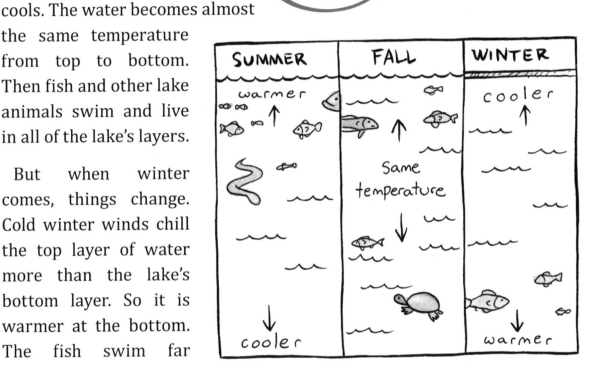

lake, which is sometimes frozen. They spend the winter in the bottom layer's warmer waters. Some creatures **hibernate** in the muddy lake bottom. When spring arrives, the water changes temperature again.

WORDS to **KNOW**

oxygen: a gas in the air that people and animals need to breathe to stay alive.

The stratification of a lake is an important process. When the water at the top and bottom of the lake is about the same temperature, the water mixes. Mixing water sends **oxygen** from the surface down to the bottom layers. It also sends nutrients and food from the bottom of the lake to the top.

Winterkill

When the layer of ice that freezes on the surface of a lake is thick enough, or is covered by snow, it can block sunlight from reaching some of the plants below. Without sunlight, these plants cannot go through the process of photosynthesis. Without photosynthesis, plants can't release oxygen into the water. And with less oxygen in the lake, some animals and plants can die. When this happens in the winter, it is called winterkill.

30

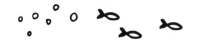

littoral zone: the area near the lake's shoreline where sunlight reaches the bottom.

shoreline: the edge of a body of water, where the water meets the land.

limnetic zone: the open water of the lake that sunlight penetrates.

profundal zone: the deepest waters of a lake where no sunlight reaches.

Did you know that a lake has different zones? The zones are based on how much sunlight they get and where they are in the lake. The **littoral zone** is near the lake's **shoreline** where the water is not deep. In the littoral zone, sunlight reaches the lake's bottom. The **limnetic zone** is the open water of the lake, away from the shore. Sunlight penetrates, or reaches into, the limnetic zone.

The deeper waters of a lake are the **profundal zone**. No sunlight penetrates the profundal zone. The amount of light that reaches different parts of a lake affects the plants and animals that live there.

Over time, lakes grow old. They fill in with sediment, plants, and algae. As dirt and debris builds up on the lake bottom, the lake becomes shallower. Over hundreds and thousands of years, a lake may fill in and disappear completely.

LIMNETIC ZONE

LITTORAL ZONE

PROFUNDAL ZONE

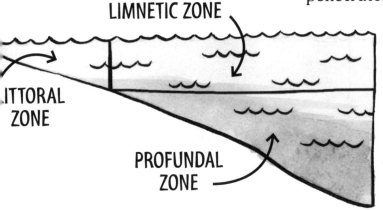

Insects in Ponds & Rivers

Have you ever been bitten by a mosquito when visiting a pond or lake? Many insects live near freshwater bodies. Some, like water beetles and water scorpions, live almost entirely in the water. They visit the surface to collect air. Other insects have special gills that get oxygen from the water. Still other insects like damselflies live in the water when they are young, but then fly above the water as adults.

WORDS to KNOW

nymph: an insect that, when hatched, looks like a tiny version of an adult.

One of the most recognizable pond insects is the dragonfly. A dragonfly starts its life as an egg in the water. Then it hatches into a wingless larva called a **nymph**. Over time, the nymph grows and sheds its skin many times. Eventually, the nymph climbs up a plant stem and sheds its skin for the last time. An adult dragonfly bursts into the air. The adult dragonflies zip around the pond eating small creatures like water insects, tadpoles, and small fish.

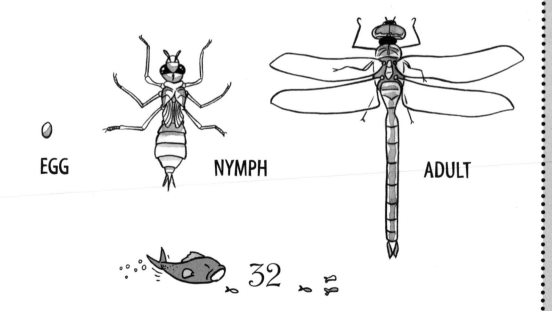

EGG   NYMPH   ADULT

Examine
Pond Ice

In the winter, ponds often freeze. Small insects and other items get stuck in the ice. What do you think you will find in your pond ice? **You must have an adult with you because you will be standing at the edge of a pond.**

SUPPLIES

- ice from a partially frozen pond
- plastic bowl
- magnifying glass
- Freshwater Journal
- pencil

1 With an adult's help, collect a few pieces of frozen pond ice from the edges of a pond. Don't walk on the ice! Make sure you stand on the ground around the pond.

2 Put the ice in your plastic bowl and take the bowl inside. Let the ice melt at room temperature.

3 Use your magnifying glass to look at the water. What do you see in the pond water? You might find tiny creatures, leaves, twigs, or other items that were on the surface when the pond froze.

4 Make a page in your Freshwater Journal called "Pond Ice" and record what you see.

Watch
Tadpoles Become Frogs

In spring, frogs lay up to 20,000 eggs in wet places like ponds and lakes. After about three weeks, frog eggs develop into tadpoles. Tadpoles have long tails and live in water. They eat very small pond plants.

After about five weeks, a tadpole begins to change into a frog. It grows back legs. Then it grows front legs. Its tail gets smaller. Inside, the tadpole begins to develop lungs so that it can breathe on land. After about 12 weeks, the tadpole becomes a frog and leaves the water to live on the land.

SUPPLIES

- container, like an aquarium, fishbowl, plastic garbage can, or garden pond
- sand or gravel
- pond plants (optional)
- water
- tadpoles from a pet store or a pond
- lettuce
- Freshwater Journal
- pencil

1 Find a container for your tadpoles. It should be shallow and wide.

2 Pour sand or gravel in the bottom of the container. If you want, you can add a few plants to help put oxygen in the water.

3 Fill your container about three-quarters full with water. Let it sit for five to seven days. This will allow any chlorine in the water to evaporate. Chlorine can kill tadpoles.

4 Add the tadpoles to your container. Put your container in a safe place where it cannot be knocked over.

5 Have an adult help you freeze or boil lettuce. Then chop or tear it into smaller pieces. Use the chopped lettuce to feed your tadpoles every day.

6 Watch your tadpoles as they change into frogs. What do you observe? Most tadpoles will change in six to eight weeks. Some take longer if it's cold outside.

7 Record your observations in your Freshwater Journal as the tadpoles begin to turn into frogs. How long does it take? What changes happen first? You may want to draw some pictures of the tadpoles as they change.

8 Once your tadpoles have become frogs, you can release them back into the pond where you collected them. If you bought them in a pet store you can release them into a healthy pond.

Make Your Own
Fishless Aquarium

Ponds are filled with tiny creatures that you might not see the first time you look. Here's a way you can discover some of these tiny creatures.

1 Take a trip to a local pond. Scoop some soil or sand from the bottom and dump it into the bucket.

2 Add some of the soil to the bottom of your glass jar. Plant a few water plants in your jar and fill it with pond water.

3 With your net, scoop pond life like snails or water insects. Add a few to your jar. If the jar is too crowded, they may die.

4 Keep your jar in a cool place, not directly in the sun. Make sure that you move or shake your jar as little as possible.

5 Over several days, observe your fishless aquarium. What creatures can you see? How do they move around? What do they eat? Are the plants growing?

6 After about a week, return the plants and animals from your fishless aquarium to the pond.

36

Make Your Own
Bug Card

Many insects live near ponds and lakes. But how do you know what type they are? Make a bug card, of course! **Ask an adult to supervise while you use the Internet.**

1 Have an adult help you use the Internet or a nature book. Research the types of insects that live in your area.

2 Draw pictures of the insects on your bug card or print out pictures of the bugs and glue them to your bug card.

3 Write the name and a short description of each bug next to its picture.

4 When you have finished, take your bug card on your next pond field trip! If you like, take your bug card to a copy center to have it laminated. This way it won't be ruined if it gets wet.

SUPPLIES
- Internet access or nature book
- piece of sturdy paper or cardstock, 8½ by 11 inches (21½ by 28 centimeters)
- fine-tip markers
- glue (optional)

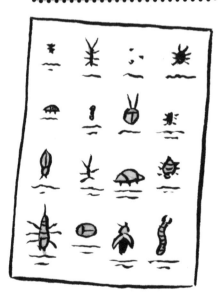

Be a Pond Inspector
And Name That Bug!

What types of living things can you find in a pond? Weeds, insects, and other tiny water creatures all live in pond water. Here's a chance to put your bug card to work!

1 Use the bucket to scoop some pond water. Use your dipping net to collect bug samples.

2 Pour your samples into the white pan. This makes it easier to see.

3 Use your magnifying glass and bug card to inspect the water and bugs. What do you see? Do any of the bugs match a bug on your card? Record them in your Freshwater Journal.

4 If you have a microscope, put some of the pond water on a slide. Study it under the microscope. Do you see any more creatures?

5 When you are finished, return the water and insects to the pond.

Become a
Freshwater Scientist

Scientists always keep track of what they find so they can learn from their experiments. Now that you've inspected water from different places, it's time to organize your results.

1 In your Journal, make 4 columns and label them Freshwater Life, Puddle, Pond Ice, and Pond Water.

2 Look back in your journal to your "Examine Life in a Puddle," experiment. List what you found in the Freshwater Life column. Make an "x" in the Puddle column for each one.

Freshwater Life	Puddle	Pond Ice	Pond Water

3 Now look back to the "Examine Pond Ice" and "Be a Pond Inspector and Name that Bug!" experiments. Add anything new to the Freshwater Life column and make an "x" in the columns for everything that you found.

4 Look at your chart and record how your experiments compare. What do they have that's the same? What is different?

Streams and Rivers

What would you see if you could you look at images of some of the world's largest rivers taken from space? You would see spidery lines that twist and turn in all directions. These are Earth's rivers and streams flowing in many shapes and sizes. Large rivers, winding streams, and tiny creeks all flow across the world's continents. Except Antarctica! You won't find any there. It might look like rivers and streams carry a lot of water, but they are only a tiny part of the earth's total surface water. Much less than 1 percent!

Where does the water in rivers and streams come from? Most of it comes from rain and snow. When rain falls, some of it soaks into the land and stays there as groundwater. Some of it evaporates. But some becomes surface runoff that flows downhill over the land until it ends up in rivers and lakes. And some groundwater seeps back into the rivers.

40

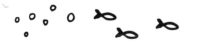 
How a Stream Becomes a River

All rivers start from a high point. They can start at the top of a mountain, hill, or other high place. The water source may be a **spring**, melting snow, or a lake. Sometimes ditches and small dry streams fill up with rainwater. Because **gravity** pulls the water downward, it flows from the high point to lower places.

WORDS to KNOW

spring: a source of water that flows out of the ground as a small stream or pool.

gravity: the force that pulls things down toward the surface of the earth.

At first, water flows downhill as a small creek. Then water from rain, snowmelt, or other places enters the creek and makes it larger. Small creeks come together to form streams. Streams join and become small rivers. Small rivers join and become medium-sized and large rivers. Large rivers eventually flow into lakes or oceans.

Up high at the river's **source**, the water is usually clean. But as water flows downstream, it picks up sediment and minerals from the soil and rock in the riverbed. Other **pollutants** like animal waste, factory waste, and farm runoff also enter river water as it flows.

WORDS to KNOW

source: where the river begins.

pollutant: something that creates pollution and harms the environment or an ecosystem.

headwaters: the streams that are the beginning of a river.

tributary: a stream or river that flows into a larger stream or river.

Parts of a River

The source of a river forms its **headwaters**. A river's headwaters can be small or large. The headwaters are important because anything that happens to them affects the entire river.

As the river flows downstream, smaller **tributaries** feed into it. When two rivers join, the larger one is the main river. The smaller one becomes the tributary. Large rivers get a lot of water from their tributaries.

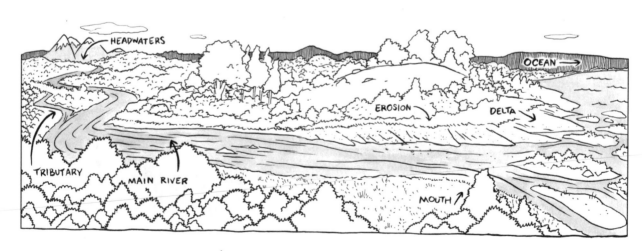

HEADWATERS

OCEAN →

EROSION

DELTA

TRIBUTARY

MAIN RIVER

MOUTH

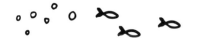 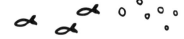

WORDS to KNOW

meander: the twisting and turning of a river's flow.

mouth: the point where a river empties into a larger body of water, like an ocean or sea.

Rivers come in many different shapes and sizes. Some are wide and straight, while others wind across the land and do not follow a straight course.

Most rivers have an upper, middle, and lower course. At the upper course, rivers move quickly and carve out rock and waterfalls. Then the river widens in the middle course, where it slows down and **meanders**. In the lower course, the river reaches the end of its journey and at its **mouth** is calm. Some rivers, like the Congo River in Africa, are powerful in the middle course, and others, like the Amazon River in South America, are strong at the mouth.

Did You Know?

About two-thirds of your drinking water comes from rivers and streams.

A River's Flow

What is a river's flow? Flow is the amount of water that flows in a river. Some rivers are large, with rushing waters. Others are small streams that dry up when rain and snowmelt run out. Sometimes a river's flow changes based on the time of year or amount of rainfall. A river's flow also depends on how the water moves through the river channel. In some natural rivers, the water flows freely. In other rivers, dams or other structures can slow or stop the water's flow.

As a river flows, it carves the land. This happens because of erosion. Over many years, rivers change the land and carve new paths. A bend in a river forms when one side of the riverbed erodes faster than the other.

WORDS to **KNOW**

riverbank: the land on either side of a river.

wildlife: animals, birds, and other living things that live wild in nature.

As rivers cut into the earth, they grind up rocks, pebbles, and soil. Over time, a river carries this debris downstream and drops it along its path. Eventually, so much soil and rock builds up that it creates new areas of land!

Did You Know?

The United States has more than 250,000 rivers. They flow more than 3.5 million river miles (5.6 million kilometers)!

Plants and trees grow along the **riverbank**. These plants and trees are an important habitat for **wildlife**. Their roots also help protect the riverbank from erosion.

Why Do Rivers Look Muddy?

Have you ever seen a muddy river after a storm? This happens because the storm's precipitation makes the river water move faster. The faster the water moves, the more dirt, rocks, and debris it can pick up from the river bottom. After a big storm, a river can actually carry more than half of all the dirt it carries in a year!

44

WORDS to KNOW

floodplain: a low area of land near a stream or river that can flood.

countershading: when an animal uses dark and light coloring to hide itself.

predator: an animal that hunts another animal for food.

Sometimes the land on either side of a river is very flat. A lot of rain or snowmelt can cause a river's water level to rise so high that it overflows onto these **floodplains**. When the water level goes back to normal, soil from the bottom of the river is left behind on the floodplain. This soil is usually rich in nutrients and makes floodplains good areas for growing food.

Animals in Ponds & Rivers: Fish

When you visit a pond or river, you might see a dark shape swimming silently beneath the water. These bodies of water are home to many freshwater fish. Some have a dark back and a shiny belly. This is called **countershading**. It helps to hide them from **predators** above and below. From above, the dark color hides the fish against the dark pond or river bottom. From below, the fish's silvery belly is hard to see against the ripples and sunlight flashes at the surface of the water.

45

WORDS to KNOW

delta: a collection of rocks and soil at the mouth of a river.

crops: plants grown for food and other uses.

When you reach the end of a river, you've arrived at its mouth, where it empties into another body of water. At the mouth of many rivers, the land flattens and forms a **delta**. Because the river moves slower at the mouth, it can no longer carry the soil and dirt that it picked up along its way. It drops the soil and dirt in the river delta and creates new areas of land. A delta can form in many shapes, but it usually spreads out in a fan shape or triangle.

The Mighty Mississippi

The Mississippi River is the third-longest river in North America. It begins at Lake Itasca in Minnesota and flows about 2,350 miles through 10 states in the center of the United States (3,782 kilometers), then empties into the Gulf of Mexico. At its widest point, the Mississippi stretches 2 miles wide (over 3 kilometers). At its headwaters, the water flows a little more than 1 mile per hour (2 kilometers per hour). That's not even half as fast as a person walks. Near the Mississippi Delta in New Orleans, the river moves faster. It flows at about 3 miles per hour (almost 5 kilometers per hour). In 2002, Martin Strel, a swimmer from Slovenia, swam the entire length of the Mississippi in 68 days!

Towns up and down the river use the Mississippi for freshwater. Many farmers live and work along the river. The river's banks are good for growing **crops**, such as grain and soybeans. Farmers also use the Mississippi River to move goods up and down the river.

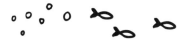 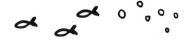
The soil in a delta is rich in nutrients and good for growing food. A river delta is also a good place for fish, birds, and other animals to live. Sometimes the material in a delta can even be thick enough to build on. The city of New Orleans, Louisiana, is built on the delta where the Mississippi River meets the Gulf of Mexico.

WORDS to KNOW

species: a group of plants or animals that are closely related and look the same.

reptile: a cold-blooded animal, like a snake or a lizard, that needs sunlight to keep warm and shade to keep cool. It crawls on its belly or on short legs.

migrate: to move from one region to another when the seasons change.

Many animals make their homes in the Mississippi River and its floodplain. The river holds at least 260 **species** of fish. More than 50 mammal species and 145 types of amphibians and **reptiles** live in the Upper Mississippi area. Birds use the river as they **migrate** north and south.

The Mississippi River has also become part of our popular culture. Mark Twain's classic book, *The Adventures of Huckleberry Finn,* journeys down the Mississippi. The popular Broadway musical *Show Boat* from the 1920s is set on a river showboat on the Mississippi. And a number of musicians like Johnny Cash and Led Zeppelin have written songs about the river.

47

Rivers Give Life

Rivers have always been important to life on Earth. Animals and plants gather around rivers for water and food. Rivers carry water and nutrients to places along the river channel. And they are a natural place for rain and surface runoff to go.

Did You Know?

It's no surprise that many cities in the world have been built along rivers. People use rivers in many ways. We drink the water. Boats and barges carry people and goods on rivers from one place to another. River water **irrigates** crops. Flowing river water generates electricity. Calm

When you move upstream in a river, you are headed toward the river's source. Paddle downstream and you'll be headed toward the river's end or mouth.

irrigate: to supply land with water, usually for crops.

WORDS to KNOW

rivers are also a great place to relax and enjoy swimming and boating. Be glad for the rivers where you live!

Make Your Own
Bark Rubbing

Trees growing along rivers and streams protect against soil erosion and provide shelter for wildlife. Depending on where you live, you might find River Birch, Quaking Aspen, Nuttall Oak, or Weeping Willow. **Have an adult supervise while you use the Internet.**

SUPPLIES
- older trees near a stream or river
- several pieces of thin drawing paper
- pushpins
- several crayon stubs with the paper peeled off
- Internet access

1 Go to a stream or river and look at the trees there. On each type of tree you see, pin a piece of paper to the tree trunk.

2 Rub the flat length of a crayon across the paper. As you rub, the bark's pattern will appear. When you are finished, remember to take out the pushpins from the trees and put them away.

3 Use the Internet to identify the species of trees from your bark rubbings.

CLASSROOM CONNECTION: Have your entire class collect bark rubbings from trees near streams and rivers. Compare the rubbings. What differences do you see? How many different types of trees did you find?

Experiment with
Water Layers

In deep rivers and lakes, the water at the bottom often feels colder than the water near the top.

SUPPLIES
- ⊙ plastic tub or sink
- ⊙ two identical balloons
- ⊙ hot water
- ⊙ cold water

1 Fill the tub or sink with cold water.

2 Fill one of the balloons almost full with hot water. Tie the end of the balloon tightly.

3 Fill the second balloon almost full with cold water. Tie the end of the balloon tightly.

4 Place each balloon in the tub of cold water. Which one sinks and which one floats?

molecule: the tiny particles that make up everything.

dense: packed tightly together.

WORDS to KNOW

HOW IT WORKS: The balloon with the hot water should float. Cold water is heavier than warm water. Its **molecules** are closer together, which makes it more **dense**. That's why the balloon with hot water floated on top of the cold water. It's is the same reason that cold water sinks to the bottom of a lake or river.

Smooth Your Own
River Rocks

Have you ever wondered why rocks in streams and rivers are smooth? This happens because the constant movement of the water wears away the rock's sharp edges.

SUPPLIES

- several small pieces of brick or rough rocks
- plastic jar with lid
- water

1 Carefully examine the edges of your brick or rock pieces. Feel how rough they are.

2 Place several pieces in the plastic jar and fill the jar with water. Seal it with the lid.

3 Shake and swirl the jar about 100 times. You may want to ask some friends or family members to help you.

4 Shake and swirl the jar another 100 times. Repeat a third time.

5 Open the jar and take out the pieces. Feel them. What differences do you notice?

HOW IT WORKS: The pieces of brick or rock should feel smoother than when you started. The swirling motion of the water and the pieces rubbing against each other wore away the rough edges. This is how the constant motion of rivers and streams creates smooth, round rocks.

Measure
Stream Speed

Streams and rivers move at different speeds. This experiment will help you find out how fast the water moves downstream. **Ask an adult to join you when you visit the stream.**

SUPPLIES
- stream
- stick
- measuring tape
- floating object such as an orange, a leaf, or a toy boat
- stopwatch

1 Go with an adult to a nearby stream or river. Use a stick to mark a spot next to the water that will be the finish line for this experiment.

2 Measure 3 feet upstream from the finish line (1 meter). How do you know which way is upstream? Notice which way the water is flowing. If you can't tell just by looking at the water, you can drop in a dry leaf to see. Upstream is where the water is coming from.

3 Drop your floating object into the stream. At the same time, start your stopwatch.

4 Click off the stopwatch when the object crosses the finish line. Do this a few times.

5 Use math to figure out the stream's speed:
3 feet (1 meter) ÷ time on your stopwatch = stream speed.

For example, if the object took 2 minutes to reach the finish line, then 3 feet ÷ 2 minutes = 1½ feet per minute. Or, if the object took 6 seconds to cross the finish line, then 3 feet ÷ 6 seconds = ½ foot per second.

River Power

Hydroelectric power uses the power of a river's flowing water to generate electricity. The river water is held behind a dam. When the water is let out, it spins the blades of a device called a turbine inside the dam. The turbines have metal coils inside that are surrounded by magnets. When the magnets spin over the coils, they produce electricity. The biggest hydroelectric dam in the United States is the Grand Coulee Dam in Washington State. It's also the largest concrete structure ever built: 5,233 feet long and 550 feet high (1,600 meters long and 168 meters high)! It has four power plants with 33 generators and makes enough electricity for more than 2 million homes.

Make Your Own
Mold of Animal Tracks

The animals that gather at rivers and ponds sometimes leave tracks or paw prints in the moist soil. If you find some tracks, you can make a permanent copy of them. **Ask an adult for help when you use a pocket knife.**

1 Visit a stream or pond. Carefully search the ground for animal tracks.

2 For each track you want to mold, put ½ cup of water into the mixing container (125 milliliters).

3 Pour 1 cup of the Plaster of Paris powder into the water for each animal track. Stir with a spoon until there are no lumps.

4 Pour the plaster into the tracks. Wait about 20 to 40 minutes for the plaster to harden. It should feel as hard as a rock when it is ready.

SUPPLIES
- measuring cups
- water
- mixing container
- Plaster of Paris powder
- spoon
- pocket knife
- small box
- paint brush

5 Have an adult carefully cut the dirt around the plaster casts with a knife and lift them gently.

6 Put the casts in the box. Let them continue to harden for several hours. Then gently brush off the dirt. You can also rinse them with water.

CLASSROOM CONNECTION: Examine all the plaster tracks. Can you figure out what animals made them?

The Ancient Nile

The Nile River has flowed through Africa for 30 million years. It is known as the world's longest river, although some scientists think the Amazon River in South America might be longer. The Nile is about 4,200 miles long (6,760 kilometers). It starts south of the equator and flows north through 10 different counties and the Sahara Desert. The Nile forms a delta in Egypt where it reaches the Mediterranean Sea. The Nile Delta is some of Africa's best land for growing crops. The Nile River **Basin** is enormous. It fills about one-tenth of the African continent, and is home to over 160 million people.

basin: an area of land drained by a river and its branches.

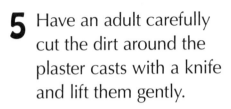

WORDS to KNOW

55

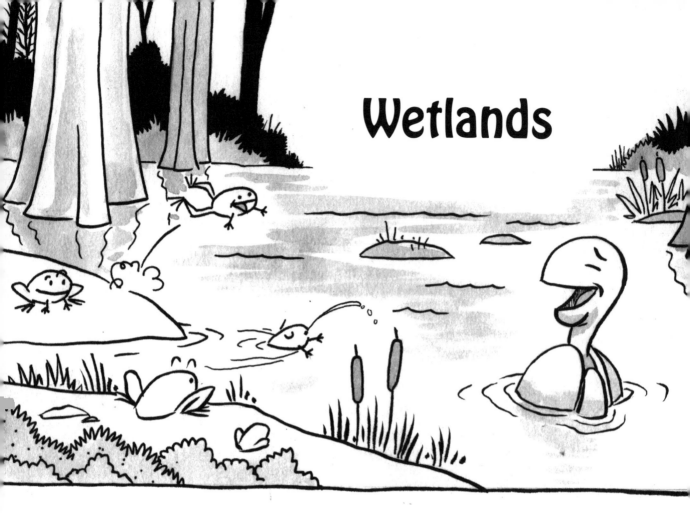

Wetlands

Do you live near a swamp, marsh, or bog? If you do, then you live near a wetland! Wetlands are important to the earth's ecosystems. The plants in wetlands are food for fish and other animals. Migrating birds stop in wetlands to rest and eat. Animals come to wetlands for food, water, and shelter.

Different types of wetlands are found all over the world. You've probably heard of swamps, marshes, and bogs. But there are others. Have you ever heard of fens, playas, and prairie potholes?

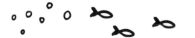 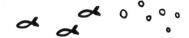
Marshes

One of the most common wetlands is a freshwater marsh. A marsh is an inland area that has between 1 and 6 feet of water (33 to 200 centimeters). Marshes are often found in low, open areas. Water from a nearby creek, stream, river, or lake flows into the marsh. Many marshes exist near the mouth of a river. In the United States, the Florida Everglades is the biggest freshwater marsh.

Water in a marsh is rich in minerals. This makes it a great place for wetland plants like cattail, sawgrass, water lily, pickerel weed, spike rush, and bulrush to thrive. In the Everglades alone, there are over 100 species of marsh plants. This rich plant life gives lots of food and shelter to animals there.

How Wet is a Wetland?

A wetland is an area that is covered or soaked with shallow water for at least part of the year. The water comes from rivers or groundwater. Some of the low-lying land of a wetland stays under water all the time. Other wetlands hold water for only a few weeks. When the water dries up, the wetlands disappear. These seasonal wetlands return when water fills them up again. The soil in wetlands doesn't have much oxygen and is wet most of the time.

You'll find fish, birds, insects, and amphibians living in a marsh. Some animals live in the water. Others, like frogs, turtles, and beavers, live on the water's surface. Raccoons and muskrats live on the soggy land around the marsh. Above the marsh, birds and insects fly from place to place. If you go to the Everglades, you'll have to keep a close eye out to find its most **endangered** species, the Florida panther.

Swamps

A swamp is a freshwater wetland that grows woody plants like trees and shrubs. This is one of the ways that a swamp is different than a marsh. The water in a swamp is also usually shallower than the water in a marsh. Mangrove or cypress trees are common woody plants in a swamp.

Swamps are often found near rivers and streams. When rivers and streams flood, the water carries nutrients from the river to the swamp. Some swamps have water all the time. Other swamps may dry out for part of the year.

Did You Know?

Wetlands are found on every continent except Antarctica.

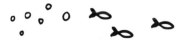
At first, a swamp may seem like a quiet, empty place. But at night the swamp comes alive with the sounds of frogs, insects, and other animals. Many forms of wildlife, like panthers, foxes, deer, and raccoons, roam near swamps. These wetlands can be dangerous places. Alligators and poisonous snakes lurk in the murky waters of swamps in the southern United States. The water is unpredictable and often changes levels. Thick, wet mud makes it difficult to move around a swamp.

Animals in Wetlands: Amphibians and Reptiles

Frogs, toads, newts, and salamanders are amphibians. When they are young, these animals live in freshwater bodies like ponds and rivers. When they become adults, they leave the water to live on land. Later in their life cycle, they return to the water to lay eggs.

Many reptiles live near ponds, rivers, and wetlands. Some, like crocodiles and turtles, live in all of these bodies of water. Others, like snakes, live in swamps, marshes, and slow-moving streams. They swim well and hunt fish, frogs, insects, and other creatures.

The Florida Everglades

The Everglades National Park is a wetland in southern Florida that covers 1½ million acres. It has many habitats that are connected by wetlands and other water bodies. There are marshes, cypress swamps, pinelands, and mangrove swamps in the Everglades.

The Everglades is known for its rich plant and animal life. Wetland plants such as sawgrass, cypress and mangrove trees, pine trees, and orchids grow in the Everglades. In some places, the sawgrass plant is so thick people call it a "river of grass." There are over 350 bird species in Everglades National Park. Large wading birds like the wood stork and great blue heron live in the Everglades. It is also the only place in the world where alligators and crocodiles live side by side. The Everglades is home to many endangered species, including the American alligator, American crocodile, sea turtles, manatees, and the Florida panther.

EVERGLADES NATIONAL PARK

conserve: to save or protect something, or to use it carefully so it isn't used up.

WORDS to **KNOW**

Today, the Everglades is just half of its original size. People have cut some of the water connections between the wetlands in the Everglades. Farms and buildings built near the Everglades have also made it smaller. Many people are working to help **conserve** and protect the Everglades.

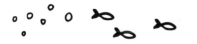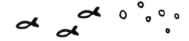
Bogs

If you only glance at a moss-covered bog, you might think it's solid land. A bog's surface looks like a carpet of spongy moss. But if you look more closely, you'll discover that underneath the spongy moss is mostly freshwater.

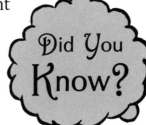

Did You Know?

A bog is a wetland that is full of peat. This is decayed plant matter that forms when plants die and fall into the water. In the United States, bogs are usually found in the Northeast and near the Great Lakes. Some are also found in the southeastern United States. A bog usually begins when moss grows over a lake or pond, slowly filling it in. Sometimes, a bog forms when moss spreads over a low area of dry land. The moss

Almost half of threatened and endangered species depend on wetlands.

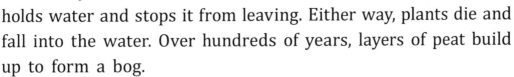

holds water and stops it from leaving. Either way, plants die and fall into the water. Over hundreds of years, layers of peat build up to form a bog.

Most of the water in a bog comes from rain. There is usually no inflow or outflow of water from a bog to another freshwater body like a lake or river. As a result, the water in a bog is usually low in the nutrients that plants need to grow.

But shrubs and evergreens grow in bogs. Bog plants like sphagnum moss, cotton grass, and cranberries have adapted to live in water with little nutrients. And the animals that stop at a bog for food, water, and shelter include moose, bear, and deer.

Prairie Potholes

Most people think a pothole is a ditch in the road. But "prairie potholes" are a type of wetland found in the northern **Great Plains**. They are shallow, sunken places out in the middle of the prairie.

WORDS to KNOW

Great Plains: a large area of flat grassland in the center of the United States between the Mississippi River and the Rocky Mountains. Another word for this grassland is prairie.

The amount of water in a prairie pothole depends on the time of year. Most prairie potholes do not hold water all year. In winter, the potholes fill with snow, and in the spring they fill with rain. Because the many potholes hold a lot of water, they help keep cities and towns in the area from flooding.

Prairie potholes are found in a part of the country that is home to more than half of all North American migrating birds. The birds use the potholes as a place for food, shelter, and nesting.

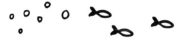

Why Are Wetlands Important?

Wetlands have several important jobs in nature. Many plants and animals live in wetlands. These species have adapted to live in a soggy, low-oxygen habitat. Even animals that live in other habitats depend on wetlands. Some animals find food and water in wetlands. For example, the heron bird nests in trees, and wades in the shallow wetlands for fish and other food. Some animals and birds find shelter in wetlands as they migrate. Others lay their eggs or raise their young in wetlands.

Wetlands also prevent flooding. They hold a lot of water, like a sponge. When storms raise water levels in rivers, wetlands absorb the extra water. This helps to keep river levels normal. When water levels are low in the rivers, wetlands slowly release their water back to the river.

recycle: to use something again.

Wetlands also help slow erosion. When river water flows, it moves sediment from one place to another. In a wetland, emergent plants have roots in the muddy bottom and rise above the water. When a river flows into a wetland, these plants slow the flow of water. Slower-moving water washes away less sediment, so erosion also slows.

Wetlands also help to clean water. This is why some people call them nature's kidneys. Your kidneys clean waste from your body. In nature, wetlands clean waste from the ecosystem. They filter sediment and dead plant matter from the water that flows to rivers. Wetlands can also **recycle** chemicals and nutrients so plants and animals can use them to grow. This makes wetlands some of the most important places in nature.

Vernal Pools

A **vernal pool** is a temporary wetland. In the spring and fall, snowmelt or rain fills a sunken place in the ground. In the winter, a vernal pool in cold climates may be covered in ice. This vernal pool usually dries up by the summer.

Because a vernal pool dries up each year, no fish live in it. Instead, insects and amphibians use vernal pools for parts of their **life cycle**. Some of the most common animals found in vernal pools are fairy shrimp, mole salamanders, and the wood frog.

Fairy shrimp live their short life cycle in the pool's water. They drop their eggs on the vernal pool bottom. The eggs remain there after the pool dries, then hatch when the water returns the next year. Wood frogs also lay their eggs in vernal pools. The eggs hatch into tadpoles. The tadpoles live in the pool while they grow into frogs. Then they follow the adult frogs into the nearby woodlands. Mole salamanders also travel to vernal pools to lay their eggs. By the time the pool dries, the eggs hatch. Then the young salamanders move to the ground to live.

Did You Know?

Some wetlands are salt water. Salt-water wetlands like salt marshes, tidal flats, and mangrove swamps are found near the ocean.

What Can You Find in a Wetland?

Wetlands hold all kinds of creatures. Take a field trip to a nearby marsh, swamp, or bog and see what you can find! **Bring an adult with you.**

1 With an adult, wade out a little bit into the water. Be very careful because the bottom of a wetland can be uneven.

2 Dig an inch or two into the dirt at the bottom of the water (2½ to 5 centimeters). Fill the bucket about halfway with the dirt and water.

3 Have a partner hold the mesh over the water. Empty a scoop of dirt and water from your bucket onto the mesh.

4 Look at what's left after the water strains through. If you don't see anything, try another scoop.

5 Return all the dirt and water back to where you found it.

CLASSROOM CONNECTION: Record in your Freshwater Journal the wetland creatures you find. Make notes, draw pictures, and share them with your class.

SUPPLIES

- ⊙ boots
- ⊙ small shovel
- ⊙ bucket
- ⊙ mesh or cheesecloth
- ⊙ Freshwater Journal
- ⊙ pencil

Experiment with
Erosion

One of the important jobs of a wetland is to slow down erosion. A wetland's plants are rooted in the soil. This helps slow the flow of water through the wetland and keeps the soil from washing away.

SUPPLIES
- sand
- soil
- aquarium or other large rectangular container
- twigs and sticks
- watering can
- water

1 Mix the sand and soil in the container and create a mound.

2 Put the twigs and sticks into only one side of the soil. They will act as trees and plants.

3 Use the watering can to water the soil. Make sure you water both sides of the mound at the same time.

4 Compare what happens to the soil on both sides. Which side had more after watering?

HOW IT WORKS: The twigs prevent some of the soil from washing away in the water. This is how the roots of trees and plants in wetlands act to slow erosion. If land is washing away from erosion, planting grass and trees there can help to stop the erosion.

Test How
Wetlands Absorb Water

Wetlands prevent flooding. Wetland soil holds a lot of water, like a sponge. This helps prevent flooding during a heavy rainstorm. Peat is in many wetland soils and is very good at absorbing water. In this activity, you will test how much water the peat absorbs and compare it to other types of soil.

SUPPLIES

- 4 coffee filters
- 4 sieves
- peat moss
- sand
- gravel
- potting soil
- 4 bowls—big enough to hold the sieve
- measuring cup
- water

1 Place a coffee filter into each sieve.

2 Fill each sieve with a different soil type—peat moss, sand, gravel, or potting soil. Place each soil-filled sieve in a bowl.

3 Pour 1 cup of water over each sieve (240 milliliters). Let each sieve sit in the bowl for about five minutes.

4 Remove each sieve from the bowl. Look to see how much water is in each bowl. Which bowl has the least amount of water? Which soil absorbed the most water?

Weave with
Cattails

You will find cattails growing in wetland areas. **Get permission to take a few for this project.**

1 After you have permission, cut several cattail leaves near their base. If you cannot find cattails for this project, you can replace them with 1-inch-wide strips of construction paper (2½ centimeters).

2 Lay several leaves vertically side by side until they are as wide as you want your mat to be.

3 Take another leaf and weave it under and over the vertical leaves.

4 Repeat with a second leaf and alternate the under and over on the vertical leaves. Make sure to keep the leaves close together as you go. You might have to adjust the leaves each time.

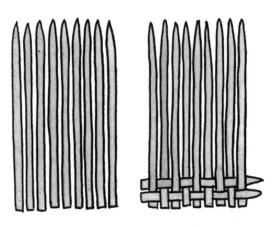

5 Continue weaving new leaves until your mat is as long as you want it. Trim the edges with scissors.

6 Press half a width of tape across the top edge of your mat. Fold the rest of the tape over to the other side of the mat. Repeat this on all four sides of your mat to help it stay in place.

Gathering Cattail Leaves

Cattails are easy to find and easy to recognize. Cattails typically grow in marshes, road ditches, ponds, swampy areas, and even in neighboring yards and around fish ponds all across the United States. They have long, narrow leaves and a brown, fluffy spike at the end of a long center stalk. This fluffy "cattail" is how the plant gets its name because it looks like the tail of a cat.

The best time to gather cattail leaves is late July, August, or early September. This is when cattails are their tallest and the tips of the leaves have just begun to turn brown. Cut the leaves at the base where they meet the water. Don't wait until the first frost to gather the leaves because they will be stiff and hard to weave!

Conservation and Protection

Without freshwater biomes, you would not be alive.
Freshwater biomes give us water for drinking.
We use their water for energy and transportation.
Freshwater is also a great place for fun like boating
and fishing. And without freshwater ecosystems,
many plants, animals, fish, and insects would
have nowhere to live, and no water to drink.

Sometimes, our freshwater lakes, rivers, and wetlands can become damaged. One of the biggest dangers to freshwater systems is pollution. Water pollution is anything that is added to a freshwater system that does not belong there. Water pollution can cause plants and animals to die. If an entire species dies, it becomes extinct.

wastewater: dirty water that has been used by people in their homes, in factories, and in other businesses.

WORDS to KNOW

fertilizer: any substance put on land to help crops grow better.

pesticide: a chemical used to kill pests such as insects.

There are many ways freshwater becomes polluted. Sometimes factories dump chemicals or **wastewater** into freshwater. Other times, rain can wash **fertilizers** from farms into freshwater. Surface runoff carries waste from farm animals into the water. **Pesticides** sprayed on farms and lawns flow into freshwater. All of these pollutants can sicken or kill a freshwater system's plants and animals.

Did You Know?

Nearly 40 percent of the rivers in the United States are too polluted for fishing and swimming.

Pollution affects lakes and rivers differently. The moving water in rivers and streams can more quickly wash away pollutants. But lakes, ponds, and wetlands cannot wash away the **contaminants** on their own. Instead, the pollution stays in these waters until people remove it or **bacteria** breaks it down. This puts lakes, ponds, and wetlands at more risk of **contamination** than rivers.

Watersheds

A watershed is an area of land with streams and rivers that drain into a larger river, lake, or the ocean. A watershed collects surface water and water seeping through the soil. As water drains through the soil, the soil acts as a filter to clean it.

WORDS to KNOW

contaminant: a material that makes something dirty or unfit for use.

bacteria: tiny organisms found in animals, plants, soil, and water. Bacteria are decomposers.

contamination: the presence of harmful substances like contaminants or pollutants in water, soil, or air.

Watersheds are especially at risk for pollution. Any pollution that is on the ground can run with surface water into the watershed. The watershed then carries the pollution into its streams and rivers. Sometimes contaminated soil erodes and washes into the watershed's streams and rivers. Other times, water draining through the ground picks up pollution that is in the soil.

The watershed's streams and rivers carry water pollution into larger rivers, lakes, and oceans. This is how pollution in one place can affect water thousands of miles away.

Other Threats

Sometimes people themselves do things that harm freshwater systems. The biggest threat to freshwater habitats is farming. But we all need the food grown on farms, right? And some crops need a lot of water. But some farmers grow crops that do not grow easily in their local climate. This means the crops need a lot of extra water, as well as pesticides, to survive. The pesticides then wash into the rest of the water and destroy the freshwater habitats.

In some places, people build dams for electricity or to store water to irrigate crops. Dams change the natural flow of rivers and streams. This disrupts the fish and other animals living in the water. People also drain wetlands so they can build on the land, which destroys wetland habitats. When people use too much freshwater for drinking and bathing, it can make freshwater habitats smaller.

Did You Know?

More than half of Earth's wetlands have been destroyed or damaged.

As freshwater habitats are damaged, some animals and plants die. Others migrate or move to nearby habitats. But when new animals move into a habitat, it can hurt the plants and animals that already live there. When animals compete for food there can be a **shortage**.

WORDS to KNOW

shortage: not enough of something for everyone.

conservation: managing and protecting natural resources.

biologist: a scientist who studies life.

Protecting Freshwater

Many people are working to help protect our lakes, rivers, and wetlands. **Conservation biologists** are scientists who try to keep freshwater systems healthy and make sure you still have enough clean water to drink. They study the plants, animals, soil, and water in a freshwater habitat. They advise people on the best ways to use freshwater resources. For example, they may study how a town that is growing can make sure it has enough clean water for everyone.

Conservation biologists also design programs to make freshwater bodies healthier. They work to protect the plants and animals that live in the freshwater biome.

Did You Know?

Scientists predict that by 2025, more than two-thirds of the world's population could face water shortages.

74

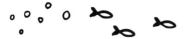
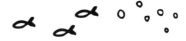

What You Can Do

There are many things you can do to help protect freshwater ecosystems. First, you can conserve water. If you use less water, there will be more water that stays in the freshwater biome. Turn off the water when you brush your teeth. Take shorter showers instead of baths. Scrape your dishes after dinner instead of rinsing them before you put them in the dishwasher.

You can also be careful about water pollution. Everything you put down the kitchen sink is part of your home's wastewater. This wastewater can eventually find its way into your freshwater. So think about what you put down the drain. Would you want to drink it? You wouldn't want grease from cars or lawn mowers, paint, nail polish remover, or medications to end up in your drinking water. Lawn chemicals can enter your watershed when rain washes over your yard. The water goes into storm drains that empty into streams, rivers, and lakes. So tell your parents that you'd rather have some weeds in your yard than pesticides in your glass!

> **restore:** to bring something back to the way it was.
>
> **WORDS to KNOW**

You can also volunteer to clean up your local freshwater habitats. Many communities have groups that work together to clean and **restore** freshwater ecosystems. Joining one of these teams will help. And you'll have a chance to see how your help makes a difference in your local sources of freshwater over time.

Measure a
Dripping Faucet

A dripping faucet doesn't seem to waste much water. But what if it dripped all day long, every day? And what if everyone in your school had a dripping faucet? Let's use math to figure out how one small drip can really add up!

1 Check your faucets at home. Do any of them drip? If yes, place your cup underneath the drip to catch the water.

2 If none of your faucets drip, pick one. Turn it on a very tiny amount so a small drip comes out at regular intervals, every few seconds or so. Place your cup underneath the faucet to catch the water.

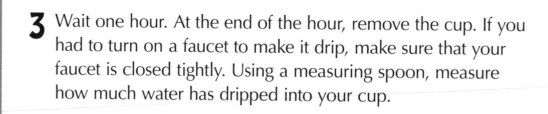

3 Wait one hour. At the end of the hour, remove the cup. If you had to turn on a faucet to make it drip, make sure that your faucet is closed tightly. Using a measuring spoon, measure how much water has dripped into your cup.

4 Now it's time for the math. You know how much the faucet dripped in one hour. How much would it drip in a whole day? That's 24 hours. **Water in 1 hour x 24 hours = water in 1 day.** Have an adult help you convert your measurement from teaspoons, cups, or milliliters to gallons or liters.

5 How much water will be wasted in a whole year? That's 365 days. **Water in 1 day x 365 days = water in 1 year.**

CLASSROOM CONNECTION: What if everyone in your school had the same dripping faucet? How much water would be wasted in a day? Multiply the amount of water dripped in a whole day times the number of kids in your school. If you want to know how much water would be wasted in a whole year by your school, multiply that amount times 365 days.

Clean Water
Naturally

A healthy watershed cleans water before it reaches a river or stream. Rain hits the earth and soaks into the ground. The ground's soil, rock, and sand filter out many of the impurities in the water. **Ask an adult to help you cut the plastic bottle.**

1 Have an adult help you cut off the bottom of the plastic bottle. Turn the bottle upside down and make sure the cap is on.

2 First, put a layer of cotton in the bottle. On top of the cotton, spread a layer of pebbles. Then add a layer of sand. Cover the sand with a layer of rocks. Then add another layer of sand. Finish with a layer of leaves. This is like the layers in the ground outside.

3 Remove the lid from the bottle. Place the bottle spout down into the mouth of a clean jar.

SUPPLIES

- plastic 2-liter bottle with cap
- scissors
- cotton
- pebbles
- sand
- rocks
- chopped up leaves
- clean jar
- bowl or container
- water
- mud

4 In a different container, mix water and mud to make dirty water. Slowly pour the dirty water into the cut-out opening of the soda bottle.

5 Watch as the dirty water soaks through the layers in your bottle. Water should drip out through the spout into your clean jar. What does it look like?

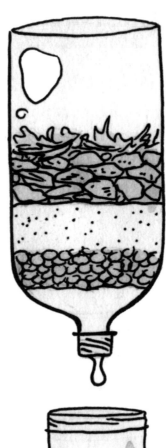

CLASSROOM CONNECTION: Do this experiment in school using different types of dirty water. Try combinations of cooking oil, food coloring, and food particles. Also try mixing up the filter system by changing the layers in the bottle to see what happens.

IMPORTANT: Do not drink the water. It will look clean, but is untested and could contain harmful bacteria.

Make a Sanctuary
for Freshwater Species

Endangered species are animals or plants that are in danger of disappearing from Earth entirely. There are only small numbers of endangered animals and plants left in the world. Many species are endangered because the places they live in are disappearing or are becoming too polluted. To help preserve endangered species, some people are working to create new freshwater habitats. **Have an adult supervise while you are on the Internet.**

SUPPLIES
- Internet access
- paper
- colored pencils

1 Look on the Internet to learn about endangered freshwater species. Find different plants and animals that live in ponds, lakes, rivers, and wetlands that are in danger of becoming extinct. You may want to use this guide to endangered species to get started: animal.discovery.com/guides/endangered/ endangered.html.

Did You Know?

In recent years, more than 20 percent of freshwater fish species have become extinct or are in danger of extinction.

2 Choose which type of sanctuary is best for the endangered species you have selected—a lake, pond, river, or wetland.

3 Using paper and colored pencils, draw a freshwater sanctuary or safe place for endangered species.

4 Add the endangered animals and plants that you have learned about to your freshwater sanctuary.

5 How are the animals and plants connected to each other? What happens if you take one away? And another?

CLASSROOM CONNECTION: Share your sanctuary with your classmates. Talk about the endangered species that you included. What endangered species did the other students include in their sanctuaries?

Learn about what you can do to help protect endangered freshwater species. The United States Fish and Wildlife Service has a web site where you can lean about their Endangered Species Program at www.fws.gov/endangered. There's even a special section called "For Kids."

Build a
Watershed Replica

A watershed is the area of land that the water in streams and rivers drains from. Watersheds can be large or small. When rain lands on the ground, it travels downhill. Eventually, the water finds its way to a stream, lake, or river.

SUPPLIES
- several rocks in different sizes
- shallow plastic tub
- sheet of plastic
- tape
- watering can
- water

1 Put the rocks in the plastic tub. Build mountains and valleys with them. Loosely cover the rocks with the plastic and tape it to the container.

2 Predict how you think water will flow in your watershed. Where will it gather or pool?

3 Using the watering can, sprinkle water on your watershed. How does it flow? Was your prediction of the water's path correct?

CLASSROOM CONNECTION: Learn about the watershed area of your school. Find your "watershed address" on the Environmental Protection Agency web site, cfpub.epa.gov/surf/locate/index.cfm. Try to figure out the path of the water that flows from your school. Where does it end up?

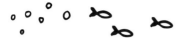

adapt: changes a plant or animal makes to live in new or different conditions.

algae: a simple organism found in water that is like a plant but without roots, stems, or leaves.

amphibian: an animal with a backbone that lives on land and in water, such as a frog, toad, or salamander. An amphibian is cold-blooded, so it needs sunlight to keep warm and shade to keep cool.

atmosphere: the air surrounding the earth.

bacteria: tiny organisms found in animals, plants, soil, and water. Bacteria are decomposers.

basin: an area of land drained by a river and its branches.

biologist: a scientist who studies life.

biome: a large area with a similar climate, and the plants and animals that live there.

bog: an area of wet, spongy land that is full of peat.

collection: when water that falls back to Earth is stored on land or in oceans, ponds, rivers, lakes, and streams.

condensation: when a gas cools and changes to a liquid.

conservation: managing and protecting natural resources.

conserve: to save or protect something, or to use it carefully so it isn't used up.

contaminant: a material that makes something dirty or unfit for use.

contamination: the presence of harmful substances like contaminants or pollutants in water, soil, or air.

countershading: when an animal uses dark and light coloring to hide itself.

course: the path of a river or stream.

crater: a large hole in the ground caused by something like a meteorite or a bomb.

crops: plants grown for food and other uses.

crustacean: a type of animal, such as a crab or lobster, that lives mainly in water. It has several pairs of legs and its body is made up of sections covered in a hard outer shell.

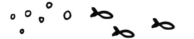 

current: the steady movement of water in one direction.

dam: a strong barrier built across a stream or river to hold back water.

debris: the scattered pieces of something that has been broken or destroyed.

decomposer: an organism, like a worm or ant, that breaks down dead and rotting organisms.

decompose: to rot or decay.

delta: a collection of rocks and soil at the mouth of a river.

dense: packed tightly together.

ecosystem: a community of living and nonliving things and their environment. Living things are plants, animals, and insects. Nonliving things are soil, rocks, and water.

emergent: a plant that is rooted in soil but has plant parts that reach above the surface of the water.

endangered: when a species is in danger of becoming extinct.

environment: a natural area with animals, plants, rocks, soil, and water.

erosion: the gradual wearing away of soil by water or wind.

evaporation: when a liquid heats up and changes to a gas.

extinct: when a group of plants or animals dies out and there are no more left in the world.

fertilizer: any substance put on land to help crops grow better.

floodplain: a low area of land near a stream or river that can flood.

flow: to move from one place to another.

food chain: a community of plants and animals, where each is eaten by another higher up in the chain.

food web: a network of connected food chains.

freshwater: water that is not salty. It is less than 1 percent salt.

glacier: a huge mass of ice and snow.

globe: a map of the earth on a round ball.

gravity: the force that pulls things down toward the surface of the earth.

Great Plains: a large area of flat grassland in the center of the United States between the Mississippi River and the Rocky Mountains. Another word for this grassland is prairie.

groundwater: water that is underground in spaces between rocks.

habitat: the natural area where a plant or animal lives.

headwaters: the streams that are the beginning of a river.

hibernate: to spend the winter in a deep sleep.

impurity: contamination or pollution.

irrigate: to supply land with water, usually for crops.

landslide: when rocks and soil slide down a mountain.

larva: the wormlike stage of an insect's life. The plural is larvae.

life cycle: the series of changes each living thing goes through from birth to death.

limnetic zone: the open water of the lake that sunlight penetrates.

littoral zone: the area near the lake's shoreline where sunlight reaches the bottom.

mammal: a type of animal, such as a human, dog, or cat. Mammals are born live, feed milk to their young, and usually have hair or fur covering most of their skin.

marsh: an inland area of wet, low land.

meander: the twisting and turning of a river's flow.

meteorite: a piece of rock from outer space that falls to Earth.

migrate: to move from one region to another when the seasons change.

mineral: something found in nature that is not an animal or plant, like gold, salt, or copper.

molecule: the tiny particles that make up everything.

mouth: the point where a river empties into a larger body of water, like an ocean or sea.

nutrients: the substances found in food that organisms need to live and grow.

nymph: an insect that, when hatched, looks like a tiny version of an adult.

organism: any living thing.

oxbow lake: a horseshoe-shaped lake that starts out as a curve in a river. It becomes a lake next to the river when the river changes its course.

oxygen: a gas in the air that people and animals need to breathe to stay alive.

peat: dark brown, partly decayed plant matter found in bogs and swamps.

pesticide: a chemical used to kill pests such as insects.

photosynthesis: the process where plants use sunlight and water to make their own food.

phytoplankton: tiny free-floating plants and plant-like organisms.

pollutant: something that creates pollution and harms the environment or an ecosystem.

pollute: to make dirty or contaminate.

pollution: harmful materials that damage the air, water, and soil. These include chemicals and factory waste.

precipitation: falling moisture in the form of rain, sleet, snow, and hail.

predator: an animal that hunts another animal for food.

primary consumer: a plant or animal that eats tiny plants and phytoplankton.

primary producer: a plant that creates its own food for energy through photosynthesis.

profundal zone: the deepest waters of a lake where no sunlight reaches.

recycle: to use something again.

reptile: a cold-blooded animal, like a snake or a lizard, that needs sunlight to keep warm and shade to keep cool. It crawls on its belly or on short legs.

restore: to bring something back to the way it was.

riverbank: the land on either side of a river.

rush: a tall plant with a hollow stem that grows in wet places like ponds and marshes.

scavenger: an animal, like a vulture or hyena, that feeds on dead and rotting organisms.

secondary consumer: an animal that eats other animals.

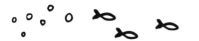 

sediment: bits of rock, sand, or dirt that has been carried to a place by water, wind, or a glacier.

shoreline: the edge of a body of water, where the water meets the land.

shortage: not enough of something for everyone.

source: where the river begins.

species: a group of plants or animals that are closely related and look the same.

spring: a source of water that flows out of the ground as a small stream or pool.

stratification: the separation of something into layers.

surface runoff: water that stays on the surface and flows into streams, rivers, lakes, and oceans.

swamp: an area of wet, spongy ground that grows woody plants like trees and shrubs.

transpiration: when plants give off moisture into the air.

tributary: a stream or river that flows into a larger stream or river.

vernal pool: a seasonal body of standing water that forms in the spring from melting snow or rain.

wastewater: dirty water that has been used by people in their homes, in factories, and in other businesses.

water cycle: the natural recycling of water through evaporation, condensation, precipitation, and collection.

waterfowl: a bird that lives on freshwater lakes and streams.

watershed: the land area that drains into a river or a lake.

water vapor: the gas form of water.

wetland: an area where the land is soaked with water, such as a swamp.

wildlife: animals, birds, and other living things that live wild in nature.

zooplankton: tiny animals that float freely in salt water and freshwater.

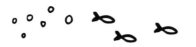

Books

Baker, Nick. *Rivers, Ponds and Lakes.* Harper Perennial, 2007.

Hooks, Gwendolyn. *Freshwater Feeders: Studying Food Webs in Freshwater.* Rourke Publishing, 2010.

Johannsen, Philip. *Lakes and Rivers: A Freshwater Web of Life.* Enslow, 2007.

Parker, Steve. *Eyewitness: Pond & River.* DK Publishing, 2011.

Yasuda, Anita. *Explore Water!* Nomad Press, 2011.

Web Sites

American Rivers
www.americanrivers.org/about-rivers/?gclid=CLXbi6fQtqwCFQaHtgodR1i2Hg

EPA—Drinking Water and Ground Water
water.epa.gov/learn/kids/drinkingwater/index.cfm

Kids Do Ecology
kids.nceas.ucsb.edu/biomes/index.html

Missouri Botanical Garden—Freshwater Ecosystems
www.mbgnet.net/fresh/index.htm

National Park Service—Mississippi River
www.nps.gov/miss/riverfacts.htm

National Wildlife Federation—The Everglades
www.nwf.org/Wildlife/Wild-Places/Everglades.aspx

U.S. Geological Survey—Water Science for Schools
ga.water.usgs.gov/edu/index.html

The Vernal Pool
www.vernalpool.org/vpinfo_1.htm

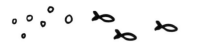
Science Museums and Aquariums

American Museum of Natural History,
New York, New York
www.amnh.org/exhibitions/water

California Science Center, Los Angeles, California
www.californiasciencecenter.org

Cold Spring Harbor Fish Hatchery and Aquarium,
Cold Spring Harbor, New York
www.cshfha.org/

Great Lakes Aquarium, Duluth, Minnesota
www.glaquarium.org/

National Aquarium, Baltimore, Maryland
www.aqua.org/

National Mississippi River Museum & Aquarium,
Dubuque, Iowa
www.mississippirivermuseum.com

The Oshkosh Public Museum, Oshkosh, Wisconsin
www.oshkoshmuseum.org/exhibits/wetlands_waterways.htm

Tennessee Aquarium, Chattanooga, Tennessee
www.tennesseeaquarium.org

University of California Museum of Paleontology,
Berkeley, California
www.ucmp.berkeley.edu/exhibits/biomes/freshwater.php

The Wetlands Institute, Stone Harbor, New Jersey
www.wetlandsinstitute.org

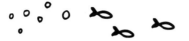 

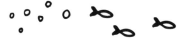 

P

photosynthesis, 9, 30
plants and trees, 2, 6, 8–13, 16, 23–25, 27–28, 30–31, 44, 48–49, 57–58, 60–63, 69–71, 74, 80–81
pollution, 3, 42, 71–73, 75
ponds and lakes, 4, 7, 8, 11, 14, 21–32, 33, 34, 36, 37, 38, 41, 50, 54, 69, 71–73
prairie potholes, 56, 62. *See also* wetlands
precipitation, 5, 7, 14. *See also* rain; snow/sleet/hail
puddles, 2, 4, 6, 20

R

rain, 7, 8, 14, 40, 43, 44, 45, 48, 61, 62, 64, 67, 71, 78, 82. *See also* precipitation
recreation, 28, 48, 70
rivers and streams, 4, 7, 8, 11, 14, 27, 40–53, 54–55, 57, 63, 71–73, 82
rocks, 7, 26, 42, 43, 44, 51, 78

S

salt water. *See* oceans and salt water
snow/sleet/hail, 7, 40, 45, 62, 64. *See also* precipitation
soil, 7, 11, 16, 24, 26, 42, 44, 45, 46, 47, 49, 54, 57, 63, 66, 67, 72, 74, 78
stratification, 28–31
streams. *See* rivers and streams
sun/sunlight, 6, 9, 15, 22, 30, 31, 45
surface runoff, 7, 40, 48, 71, 72
swamps, 4, 8, 23, 58–60, 69. *See also* wetlands

T

temperature, 6, 12, 22, 28–31, 50
transpiration, 6, 16
transportation, 47, 48, 70

U

vernal pools, 64. *See also* wetlands

W

water cycle, 5–7, 14–15, 16
watersheds, 25, 72–73, 78, 82
water vapor, 6–7, 8, 14, 16
wetlands, 2, 4, 8, 11, 23, 56–64, 66, 67, 68–69, 71–72, 73
winterkill, 30